The Character Jug Collectors Handbook

by

Kevin Pearson MBA BA(Hons)

Edited by F J Salmon BA(Hons)

Published in the United Kingdom by
Kevin Francis Publishing Company Limited,
153 Battersea Rise, London SW11
under licence from Cresswell Publications.

Typeset by SDM Typesetting Ltd, and printed in England by
The Greenwich Press, London SE7.

Acknowledgements
Derek and Jean, Gary and Jill, Adrian McKeown, Gary Sirett, Nina, Leon, Trish and Barbara, Tom Power, Syd Gardner, Dick Nicholson, John, My Fair Lady, Nick, Eric Hemmings, George Yapp, Louise Irvine, Lee Ellis, Francis Salmon, Geoff Bell, Phillips, Abridge Auctions, Peter Wilson & Co, Sothebys, Christies, Louise Taylors, California Doulton Fair Organisers, Royal Doulton International Collectors Club.

Important Notice
All the information and valuations have been compiled from reliable sources and every effort has been made to eliminate errors and questionable data. Nevertheless the possibility of error always exists. The publisher and author will not be held responsible for losses which may occur in the purchase, sale or other transaction of items because of information contained herein. Readers who feel they have discovered errors are invited to WRITE and inform us so that these may be corrected in subsequent editions.

Additional Copies
Further copies of this booklet can be obtained by ordering direct from Cresswell Publishing, Standard House, 107-115 Eastmoor Street, London SE7 8LX. Cheques/PO for £8.25 plus 60p p&p should be made payable to Cresswell Publishing. Overseas buyers should add £1 for p&p.

Any reader who wishes to contact the author for further information on character jugs should write via the publishers address.

Second Issue
Kevin Francis Publishing Company Limited

CONTENTS

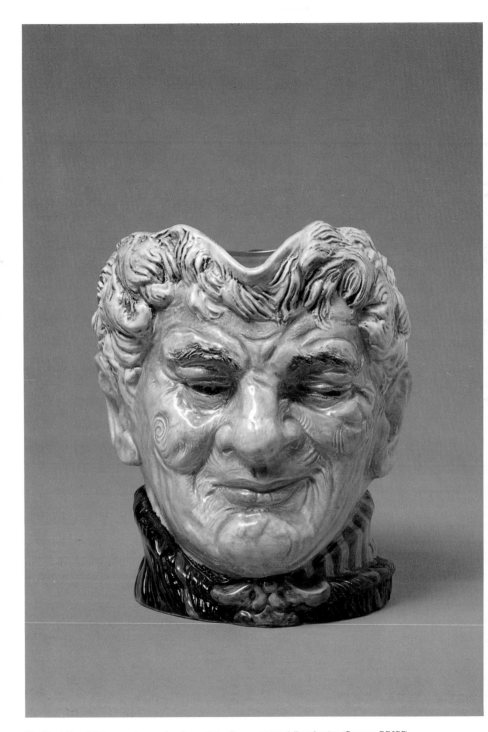

The Maori. One of the two versions produced as a pilot and never put into full production. (Courtesy RDICC)

Introduction
by the Author

Welcome to the second edition of the 'Character Jug Collectors Handbook'. Those of you who purchased the first edition will notice several additions and improvements in this edition. We have included for the first time a full listing and valuations for Doulton Toby Jugs as well as a full listing of all character jug derivities. Also included are the full results of our survey amongst readers to determine the most 'popular' character jugs. The major change, however, is to include USA market values in Dollars as well as British market values in Sterling. This has been in response to collectors suggestions from North America. The two values used for each discontinued jug are not based on any exchange rate but are based on recorded sales by Dealers and Auctions both in Britain and North America. They are as accurate as can be in a market which is constantly changing, as well as varying enormously geographically. Collectors should always bear in mind that there exists no fixed value for any piece of Doulton, since this depends solely upon the individual circumstances of the sale. Therefore, only use this guide as a source of advice, and always try to check other sources of information for current market values before purchasing an item of Doulton. Remember the only true value of a character jug is that placed upon it by the individual collector seeking to acquire it.

Throughout the Doulton collecting world which comprises Australia, Britain, North America, South Africa and New Zealand, there has been another year of growth in discontinued character jug prices. There are two reasons for this, the increasing rarity of good discontinued jugs and the growth in the number of collectors. This price rise should continue steadily especially amongst the rare middle value character jugs. 1984 saw the record price paid for any Doulton Character Jug, £14,500 plus auctioneers commission — for the Toby Gillette Jug (full story inside). Doulton Character Jugs are now more firmly than ever established worldwide as valuable art, with several major auction houses holding specialist Doulton sales and many full time specialist Doulton dealers in existence. It's difficult to estimate the number of collectors that exist worldwide however, but it probably exceeds 9,500 as the Antagonist limited edition of 9,500 jugs sold out immediately and it now attracts a premium of 50% above its issue price.

At the close of the introduction last year, collectors were wished good luck in using the prices contained in the book to spot bargains. I'm delighted to say several collectors were very fortunate indeed in doing this. Part of the fun in collecting Doulton is using your specialist knowledge to spot and acquire bargains. I'm sure most collectors have picked up a bargain or two. Here are some of the stories I have heard in the last year.

A miniature Trapper and Lumberjack were bought from a major London Auction House for ten pounds each, and incredibly resold for £1,400 a piece ($1,650). One collector picked up 5 tinies for £1 each from a flea market, whilst another bought the miniature Gulliver and Ugly Duchess for £7 each (total value approx. £500), and a slightly damaged Large Samuel Johnson for £3. One sharp eyed collector bought from a dealer a miniature Arry for £35 which turned out to be a miniature Pearly Boy valued at £250.

Doubtless to say several other bargains were acquired by collectors. I hope this second edition enables a few others to be spotted and acts as a useful guide to collectors.

How to Use This Book

This booklet, as well as being a source of information on discontinued character jugs, is also designed to enable collectors to keep accurate records of their collection. There are two quick reference lists for current and discontinued jugs. In addition to this, all the discontinued jugs are given a further listing in the market value section. In this section each jug is listed with its individual details in the manner shown below:

Tony Weller in all four sizes including extra large

Tony Weller

The father of Sam Weller in the Dickens' novel "Pickwick Papers"

Size	D. Number	Production Dates	Market Value £	Market Value $	Date Acquired	Price Paid	
Extra Large		1936-	£120-£150	$225-$250	_____	_____	☐
Large	5531	1936-60	£65-£70	$140-$150	_____	_____	☐
Small	5530	1936-60	£35-£40	$70-$80	_____	_____	☐
Miniature	6044	1939-60	£30-£35	$60-$70	_____	_____	☐

The boxed space can be ticked to indicate the purchase of a character jug, the date and amount paid to be written in the lined space. This should help collectors avoid buying duplicates by accident, as well as providing a record of their collection. The market value listed for each character jug is intended as a guide only; the actual value put on a jug rests with the collector. There are several blank pages at the end of this booklet which will be useful for notes. Collectors may find it useful to use these pages for recording auction dates and dealer's telephone numbers, etc.

Royal Doulton Character Jugs

In the 1930's Charles J. Noke, the then Art Director of Royal Doulton, modelled his design for a pitcher with a face. This was entitled 'John Barleycorn' and represented an imaginary character which signified whiskey. It was the first character jug to be produced by Royal Doulton. Shortly after its introduction the series was expanded by adding the following characters; 'Sairy Gamp', 'Old Charley', 'Parson Brown' and 'Dick Turpin'. These character jugs proved to be popular with the public and new characters were gradually added over the years. All of them were modelled on real or fictional characters from song, literature, legend and history. They range in size from 1½ to 8 inches and exhibit a diverse range of colours, styles and, of course characters. By the end of 1985 Royal Doulton will have created and produced 166 different characters, 104 of which are now discontinued across 7 different jug sizes, leaving over 250 different character jugs for the dedicated collector to persue.

Originally nearly all the characters were British, but as the series has grown in popularity worldwide, other characters from different countries, particularly the USA have been introduced. Character jugs are now a very popular Doulton line and their appeal to the general public and new collectors is still growing. New character jugs are still being issued by Royal Doulton whilst many characters have now been in continuous production for over twenty five years. In the last two years Royal Doulton have introduced limited editions of 9500 in the antagonist collection, and plan to introduce another limited series of 9500 called the 'Star Crossed Lovers'. These limited editions have, despite being priced at a premium, quickly sold out and have risen in value by over fifty percent indicating that at least 12000 collectors exist worldwide. In the last year with the withdrawal of Captain Ahab, Royal Doulton have continued their practice of occasionally withdrawing characters to make way for new models.

Bearing in mind the increasing populariry of character jugs as 'collectors items' I would expect all future withdrawals to rise in value once discontinued, as has been the case for the last five years.

Discontinued Character Jugs

The first withdrawals in the series began in the early 1940's with 'Winston Churchill'. This is a large character jug and is currently valued at about £6,000 in the British market and $10,000 on the USA market. It is now one of the most valuable and sought after of all the discontinued jugs. There is an interesting rumour about its withdrawal. Apparently, due to the unflattering image of the jug, it was discreetly suggested to the then Chairman of Royal Doulton that it should be withdrawn. Whether this request was made by Winston Churchill himself is open to speculation, but nevertheless, it was withdrawn. It seems unlikely that this was done because of poor sales when Churchill was at the height of his popularity as Britain's war leader.

Whatever the reason behind this first withdrawal in the series, other withdrawals gradually followed and by 1960, nine characters had been withdrawn, including all the intermediate size jugs. In 1960 a relatively large number of jugs were withdrawn simultaneously. The 31 withdrawals that year covered all sizes of character jugs, including the currently much sought after 'tinies'. In the late 1960's and early '70's a further 'group' of character jugs was withdrawn. This 'group' had first been issued in the early/mid 1960's and only produced for five or six years. These particular withdrawals such as 'Ard of 'Earing are now considered to be extremely rare. They can command up to nine or ten times the price of the 1960 withdrawals as their production lifetime was much shorter; in addition to this, their poor sales at the time both limited the number produced and led to their eventual withdrawal.

The early and mid 1970's was a relatively quiet period with only a few characters withdrawn. The last five years have, with the exception of 1984's single withdrawal, seen several characters withdrawn each year. This will have been due to the number of character jugs introduced over the same period. All the withdrawals in the last four years have increased in value over the existing retail price of current character jugs, in some sizes by over one hundred percent. A pattern has now been established, which means that as Royal Doulton announces a withdrawal (usually through the International Collectors Club) the shops rapidly empty of all the existing stock. This jug then reappears two months later on antique dealers stands at a premium of at least twenty per cent. The growth in value thereafter totally depends upon the Doulton market which cannot be predicted, though to date all the recently discontinued jugs have grown in value each year.

A group containing 22 of the 27 characters withdrawn by Royal Doulton in the last five years.

British Market Report

'Ard of 'Earing. (Courtesy S & G Antiques)

The White Hair Clown. (Courtesy Tom Power)

1984 has seen rise in value for all discontinued character jugs on the British Doulton market. Listed below are a few jugs with values from this edition and last years edition as a comparison.

	1984	1985	% increase
Miniature Ard of Earing	£500-£600	£700-£900	50
Auld Mac Musical Jug	£125-£175	£400-£500	185
Large Ugly Duchess	£190-£220	£260-£300	36
Small Scaramouche	£160-£190	£260-£320	40
Large White Hair Clown	£450-£500	£600-£800	60
Large John Peel	£58-£63	£65-£70	11
Miniature Mr. Micawber	£27-£31	£30-£35	13
Small Jarge	£75-£85	£125-£150	76
Intermediate Fat Boy	£70-£80	£85-£95	18
Large Lumberjack	£23-£26	£30-£34	34
Small Mephistopheles	£450-£500	£750-£800	70
Smuts	£700-£1000	£950-£1100	20
Miniature Fortune Teller	£150-£180	£210-£240	33
Mini Bust Buz Fuz	£28-£34	£35-£45	32
Toothless Granny	£350-£400	£800-£1000	150

As can be seen from the above list the rise in values has by no means been equal for all jugs varying as it does from 11% to 185%. Certain groups of character jugs have risen more quickly than others. The 1960's jugs for example are 25% to 50% higher and all miscellaneous wares have leapt ahead, particularly musical character jugs. One reason for this growth in value has been the fall in the value of the pound. This has stimulated the demand from American dealers whose buying strength has forced prices up. There has also been an increase in the popularity of jugs amongst collectors in general which has also forced prices upwards. Prices in the UK should continue to rise although not quite at the rate we have seen over the last year. This of course will depend upon several factors, one of the most important being the exchange rate, another being continued growth in the number of collectors.

The North America Market

The North American discontinued Doulton market comprising the USA and Canada is distinctly different to that of the UK. When one considers that Great Britain could be comfortably dropped into one of the Great Lakes, one of the reasons for the difference is readily apparent. The sheer size of N. America has resulted in the discontinued Doulton market being essentially mail order. Doulton does turn up in antique fairs, flea markets and antique shops in the same way as it does in Britain. However one will not have a great deal of choice unless contact is made with some of the 20 odd specialist Doulton dealers who dominate the N. America market. Due to the great distances involved most Doulton Dealers use a mailing list for distributing their "for sale and wants" lists amongst collectors. Apart from buying through the post or relying on the occasional "find" the other option is to attend one of the specialist Doulton Fairs which exist in the USA. There are three fairs scheduled for 1985 in New Jersey, Ohio and California, whilst others are being planned for 1986. These fairs run for three days over a weekend starting on a Friday evening. They usually have lectures on aspects of Doulton as well as a timetable of social events such as the Character Jug Collectors breakfast held at the recent Californian Fair. The amount of Doulton displayed for sale at these fairs has to be seen to be believed. It is not unusual for two or three versions of the rarer Doulton items to be offered for sale at the same time.

The price differential between the UK and N. America is generally in the order of 25 per cent for character jugs and as much as 100 per cent for figures. One explanation for this difference is the relative age of the each market. The USA was the first country where Doulton collecting "took off". As such the collecting fever has built up higher than anywhere else and consequently prices have developed further. The greatest private collections of Doulton are to be found in the USA and apparently at least two individual collectors have the ambition and resources, to own an example of every figure and character jug produced by Doulton.

Within the USA prices on the East Coast seem to be slightly higher than on the West Coast. The USA market is also stronger than the Canadian, leading again to higher values in the USA market. In North America in the last few years the prices for discontinued figures has remained relatively steady whilst character jug values have grown by at least 10 per cent a year, a figure which is well below the rate of growth in the UK market.

Of interest to character jug collectors is the existance of two separate character jug collectors clubs in North America, one based in California and the other in Ontario, Canada. Both these clubs issue regular informative newsletters and accept overseas collectors. For further information write to:

Character Jug Chapter
Box 5000
Caledon
Ontario LON ICO
Canada

Jug Collector
PO Box 91748
Long Beach
California 90809
USA

A report from D. Nicholson from the Canadian Character Jug Newsletter on the N. American market

Popular as character jugs may be in the UK, their popularity in North America, particularly over the past decade, is nothing short of phenomenal. Three major US conventions — combining lectures, sales and fellowship — now see collectors converge from throughout the US and Canada. The market is further served by numerous price guides and related reference books, as well as national branches of the RDICC, and, more recently, two specialisted character jug periodicals.

In the early eighties North American collectors saw an increase of over 100 per cent in the suggested retail prices of current jugs. While this certainly did not deter collectors, it may well have increased demand for discontinued jugs in that many collectors — who previously considered discontinued prices out of their range — with this increase redirected their purchasing to discontinued jugs. The zealous efforts of collectors to complete their collections have resulted in the rarer and those less available jugs — i.e. the Sixties jugs — steadily increasing in value, with the more common pieces maintaining their values or only marginally increasing. Probably the jug which has risen most dramatically is Regency Beau, which now often rivals 'Ard of 'Earing in both desirability and price. White jugs remain popular with both American and Canadian collectors, usually priced some 70-100 per cent more than their standard coloured counterparts. Whichever theory one accepts as to their origins, the demand seems based on both their oddity and lack of availability. Jug derivatives, including lighters, tobacco jars, teapots, ashpots, et al, are perhaps most popular in the US, with some collectors specialising in just these items.

Colour and backstamp remain significant considerations for many collectors, some preferring 'A' mark backstamps, others specific production years, some preferring dark complexions, others light.

One of the more interesting jugs which did not reflect the general trend, was the recent special commission Ronald Reagan. At $500 each and with a production of 5000, this jug failed to generate the anticipated demand to the extent that these jugs are now being sold off at just slightly more than half their original price. The consensus seems to be that the high price, large production and political overtones combined to make this one of the less successful special commission pieces.

While prices vary moderately throughout regions of the US and Canada, the various price guides have standardised pricing to a large extent. No longer is the tireless collector likely to discover a bargain priced Toothless Granny at a local garage sale — more likely he will discover an overpriced Falconer. As jugs have become harder to find at local shops, antique shows, markets and auctions, many collectors have regularly begun, as British collectors are undoubtedly all too aware, going farther afield.

The Reagan Character Jug. (Courtesy RDICC)

How Character Jugs are Made

Ever since the first character jugs were issued in the 1930's, Royal Doulton Character Jugs have had a reputation for quality. This could be due to the time consuming nature of the production processes involved.

The original artist first sketches the selected character in colour, and on the basis of this design, a master mould is made. From this 'master', a second working mould is made, which in turn may have up to thirty pouring moulds made from it. These moulds are only used 25-30 times, ensuring the quality of each individual jug produced. These pouring moulds are used to cast the jug which is then removed and filed down to avoid seams. The handle which is cast separately is then stuck to the main body of the jug. The completed jug then undergoes its first firing. After careful inspection to remove any flawed jugs, they are then sent to the decorating studios. At the studios the jugs are hand-painted in the colours indicated in the original sketched design. The painted jug is then fired again to harden the colours. They are then dipped in a special solution and fired for the last time to produce the glossy finish. During the late 1960's and early 70's, some jugs were made of china instead of earthenware and have the translucent appearance of fine china. In the firing process a jug will shrink by up to $12\frac{1}{2}$ per cent. The slightly uneven nature of this shrinkage process has resulted in very slight variations in size to jugs of the same character. The fine china jugs are noticeably smaller when compared to earthenware jugs.

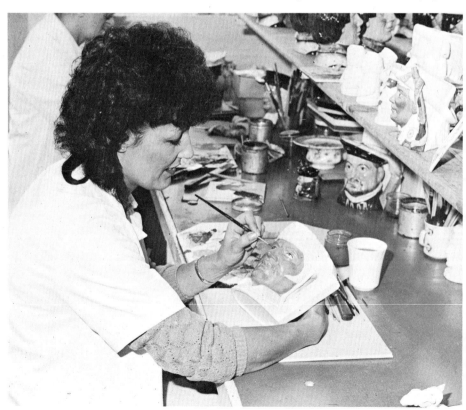

A Doulton painter at work on a newly fired jug.

Professional Restorations

Both of these jugs have been restored John Peel on the top edge of his hat and the Gondolier around his hat rim.

With the value of discontinued character jugs having risen tremendously over the last few years, there has been a corresponding rise in the number of professionally restored jugs appearing on the market. The jugs listed below show the 1977 and 1984 North American market price which has been taken from a recent Character Jug Collectors Club Newsletter.

	1977	1984	%
Min. Ard of Earing	$350	$1500	328
Large Red Hair Clown	$1800	$6000	233
Large Farmer John	$125	$165	32
Large Smuts	$950	$2300	142
Small Jarge	$125	$195	56
Large Mephistopheles	$750	$2500	233
Large Town Cryer	$80	$225	181
Large Ugly Duchess	$110	$375	240

It is a similar story in the UK where most character jugs have risen in value by 100% in the last three years.

These higher prices now make it financially worthwhile to have badly damaged character jugs professionally restored. Many of these restorations are virtually undetectable to the naked eye and are only visible under an infra red lamp. They can be detected by tapping a coin, or similar object, around the side and edges of a jug. If a jug has been restored, the repaired area will give off a slightly different sound and vibration when tapped.

Any reputable dealer will guarantee, if asked, that a jug is perfect and will refund the money if a jug is proved to be a restoration after being purchased. To avoid later misunderstanding it is always wise to ask for this verbal guarantee.

Professional restorations (especially the rare jugs) do have a market value and sell well if priced accordingly. Many collectors will buy a 'good' restoration for their collection. This is done either to reduce the cost of collecting or to enhance the collection until a perfect model of the jug can be found. The price of a restoration depends upon the quality and detectability of the restoration; as a general guide expect to pay 50-60% below the market value of a perfect version, although a particularly rare restored jug could fetch 70-80% of its perfect market value.

White Jugs

These are uncoloured character jugs, i.e only part of the glazing process has been carried out. Nearly all the examples found have some slight damage, usually underglaze chips or cracks. However perfect examples do turn up.

There are three possible reasons for the existence of whiteware pieces on the Doulton market. From 1945-1952 according to the chairman of Doulton & Co. USA, William Carry, it was official policy due to rationing regulations on decorated ware to sell whiteware pieces only on the British Market. Since 1952 other whiteware pieces have turned up, usually thought to be factory seconds that have slipped out of the factory. Another theory suggests that some seconds may have been sold to Doulton's employees in the factory shop.

Whiteware pieces are far rarer than their coloured counterparts and in the UK, after previously being valued at a slightly lower price than coloured jugs they are now valued on a par. In the USA they are viewed as being of higher value although the range of damage present in white jugs makes it impossible to estimate exact values.

Trademark Identification and Dating

Each Royal Doulton Character Jug carries the Royal Doulton lion and crown back-stamp on its base with the character's name (except for tinies) written on the back of the jug. Models may carry a copyright registration date and a D. number as well. There may be several registration numbers on the base of a jug (differing for various countries in which the design has been registered). The only mark on the bottom of a jug which may affect its value if not present is the omission of the lion and crown back stamp. The appearance or non appearance of names, registration dates and D. numbers does not affect a character jugs value.

Character jugs that have only been in production for a few years can easily be dated from production records. If the jug has been in production over a longer period, the dating process is not so simple. To an experienced collector, the quality and strength of individual colours can be an indication of age. In addition to this, older jugs quite often have a colouring on the lip inside the top of the jug, this practice ceased in 1959. The old versions can also be identified if the base bears the words, 'Reg. applied for', or has only one registered design number. This is the British registration. The first jugs of a new character were always registered and sold in Britain prior to being sold overseas.

14

Jugs that have their names printed in inverted commas, with or without a registration number, date after the previously mentioned marks. Jugs produced after 1950 have the printed name, D. number and several registered numbers on their base. Up to the mid 50s character jugs were produced with indented pupils in their eyes. Jugs produced after this period have smooth rounded eyes.

On the base of some jugs there appears what is called an "A" mark, a capital letter A printed next to the Doulton trade mark. The "A" mark appears on a range of Doulton products made between 1939 and 1955. This mark was used only as a factory control mark to direct wares to a certain kiln. It does not appear on all the character jugs made during this period, and it is of little use for the precise dating of a character jug. On the American discontinued character jug market however, the A mark jugs command a slightly higher price than non A mark jugs.

Early character jugs can be precisely dated if there is a printed numeral to the right of lion and crown. This numbering system (which also applies to figures and other items) began with the number '1' in 1928 and ran to number 27 in 1954 but was only applied sporadically. Where they do appear, a simple rule is to add the number to 1927 so a 13 would indicate 1940.

There are variations in backstamps which avid collectors will pay a premium for. "Mephistopheles" occasionally carries a quotation about the devil by Rabelies. For King George and Queen Mary's Silver Jubilee in 1935, small size "Simon the Cellarer", "Old Charley", "Sairey Gamp", "Tony Wellor" and "Parson Brown", jugs were commissioned with a special Jubilee backstamp by Bentalls Ltd. In 1967 "North American Indian" and "Trapper" were sold only in North America and carried a special backstamp which included the words "Canadian Centennial Series 1867-1967". When the jugs were issued worldwide in 1968 this backstamp was removed. "W. C. Fields" and "Mae West" were initially commissioned by American Express and a small number exist with an Amex backstamp. "The Fireman" also exists with a special backstamp of Griffith's Pottery in the U.S.A.

Character Jug Handle Variations

Handles do exhibit the same diversification, creativity and occasional rare valuable variations as jugs themselves. The first character jugs produced in the 1930's generally had very plain utilitarian handles. There were exceptions however, both "Smuts" with its springbok's head built into the back of the handle and "The Clowns" have rich colourful handles, while "Simon the Cellerar" has a handle in the form of a bunch of keys and "Dick Turpin" has a gun for a handle. "Touchstone" introduced in 1936 has two comic masks built into its handle giving a very pleasant look to the jug. Other early jugs were not so decorative, for example: "Mr. Micawber" and "Mr. Pickwick" are amongst others which simply have plain black handles coming out of their side or back. This shortage of "good" handles amongst the early jugs is well illustrated by the twelve tinies. Although introduced at a later date all the characters in the tinies are amongst the first produced in other sizes. Of the twelve characters used, only two, "John Peel" with his riding crop and "Sairey Gamp" with her umbrella had handles which reflected and continued the story of the character.

Simon the Cellarer's key, Mr Quakers sheaf of corn, The White Hair Clown.

The 1950's with the introduction of such jugs as "Rip Van Winkle", "The Poacher" and "Don Quixote" signalled a start by the Doulton designers to pay greater attention to and exploit the creative potential of character jug handles. The ten 1960's introductions and subsequent withdrawals such as "Ard of Earing" with its handle in the form of a cupped hand to his ear and the "Ugly Duchess" with her flamingo handle are for my money, some of the most pleasing and interesting of all the 90 odd jugs produced to date. "The Ugly Duchess" handle is particularly attractive to me for its artistic style and also the thought behind it shown by using a bird associated with the Duchess in the classic "Alice in Wonderland". Other jugs have featured animals as handles. Examples are, Captain Ahab's whale, Gone Away's fox, Long John Silver's parrot and St. George's dragon to name but a few. Other handles have depicted objects associated with the main character such as The Jockey's winning post, The Mikado's fan, The Gondolier's boat, and The Gladiator's dagger. The astrological symbols on The Fortune Teller's handle and the Star of David, an old magic symbol on Merlin's handle are examples of associated symbols being used. Quite often a handle will depict more than one object associated with the character; Captain Hook's alligator and clock, Robinson Crusoe's palm tree and Man Friday are examples. An even more intricate design is the "Gulliver" handle which has two Lilliputians from the story of "Gullivers Travels" attempting to lift a hair from the jugs head.

From these and other examples of handles we can see the creative potential possible in character jug handles. Once one has settled on the main design for a jug there are endless variations possible, a fact recently exploited by designer Michael Abberley in his "Santa Claus" character jug, which has been issued with a different handle every Christmas for the last three years. Given the potential of this concept one wonders whether or not future jugs might occasionally follow this.

Two views of different Beefeater handles. The first being the plain GR version and the second the newly discovered yellow crown handle.

There are in a few cases slight variations in the handles of the same jugs, several of which make a great difference to the value. In a few cases this difference in value can be as high as 1000 percent. "Anne of Cleves" is a good example of this. The handle of this jug is in the shape of a horse. Early versions in 1980 had the horse's ears upright, sticking out from its head. Due to an unacceptably high percentage of ears breaking off during transit, the ears were remodelled to be flat on the horses head. This early version now commands a premium price from collectors seeking to acquire it.

A similar situation occurred with the miniature size "Old Salt". First introduced in the large and small size in 1961, the jug has a handle in the form of a mermaid. Her outside arm is raised with her hand holding the back of her head and a noticeable space in the crook of her arm. When the miniature size was introduced in 1983, this space was no longer present because of similar problems caused during firing, i.e. the arm kept snapping off. However, a limited number were apparently piloted with the space in the crook of her arm still present; these occasionally do turn up and are avidly sought after by keen collectors.

"The Beafeater" jug has a rich variety of handles. First introduced in 1947 the back of the handle carried the initials 'GR' (George Rex), signifiying the Beafeaters status as a member of the royal household of King George. When Queen Elizabeth ascended the throne in 1953, the initials were changed to 'ER' (Elizabeth Regina), representing the new monarch. No doubt when Prince Charles ascends the throne, the jug, if still produced will change its initials once again to 'CR' (Charles Rex). The early 'GR' version does command a slightly higher value than the current 'ER' version. In addition to the initial's variations, there also exists another version known as the gold handle "Beafeater". In this version the handle is very colourful with an intricate gold thread pattern on it. Needless to say, this version is very valuable and highly sought after.

17

Other handle variations which do not make too much difference in value also exist. "John Barleycorn", the first character jug ever produced, has a very plain handle which does not depict any aspect of the jugs character. It is possible to identify early versions of the jug by a slight difference in the handle; the later version has both ends of the handle stuck to the side of the jug while the early versions have the top end of the handle disappearing into the top of the jug. "Sairey Gamp" has in early large versions a S etched at the bottom of its handle. "The Fireman" has been produced with three different coloured handles, metallic, yellow and orange, the metallic being a pilot version. John Peel's handle in the form of a hunting crop has a coloured band just below the corner of the handle. Two colours were used, orange and grey, the grey being the more common of the two, yet no real difference in value exists between the two versions. Another interesting variation occurs in the "John Doulton" jug issued by The Collectors Club; the clock face incorporated into the handle either reads two or eight o'clock. Collectors who have the 8 o'clock version are founder members of the club, whilst those with the 2 o'clock version joined at a later date. The time was apparently changed after the launch period. There is also a slight variation in the miniature "Mr. Micawber" where the handle comes out of the side of the jug instead of the back. It also has a slightly different expression around its mouth. There again, no difference in value is attached to this version, although it is of interest to the true collector.

So take a good look at the handles in your collection. Maybe you have the rare miniature "Old Salt" or an early "Anne of Cleves" or have you another variation not yet known about? Good luck in checking those handles.

Valuing Collections

This booklet will only give the approximate replacement value of a collection, not it's selling value, which could be considerably lower. The only way to sell a collection at it's replacement value is to sell it to another collector prepared to pay the market price. If this is not possible, the only alternatives are to sell the whole collection to a Doulton Character Jug dealer, or through an auctioneer. A reputable dealer will pay 15% to 30% below the price which he/she feels that they can obtain by reselling the character jugs. The price offered will vary according to the size of the collection and the individual dealer.

The great advantage of selling to dealers is the speed at which hard cash can be raised from part, or all, of a collection. Alternatively, collections or individual jugs can be sold through auctions. In this case there is no guarantee as to the exact price the jug will reach and the auctioneers commission (usually about 15% will be deducted from the amount raised. Goods are required to be entered for auction some weeks before the auction date and cheques will not be issued until one or two weeks after the sale takes place. A minimum price can be set for each jug which ensures that it will not be sold below this price, but a percentage of this price will usually be charged if the owner is unable to sell. However, as previously stated, auctions can produce a price that is well above the open market price.

Rarities

As the title suggests the purpose of this section is to illustrate that group of Character Jugs which are so rare that their market value outstrips all other discontinued Character Jugs. In most cases these jugs are what is known as 'pilot jugs'. They are prototypes of jugs that did not go into production and somehow escaped onto the market. Other rarities are mould variations on characters subsequently produced over a number of years or jugs produced in very limited numbers for one reason or another. Market values when possible are given, but many of these jugs are so rare they rarely if ever appear in the market and subsequently are impossible to value.

Red, White and Brown Hair Clowns
Excepting the brown variation, red and white hair clowns are neither pilots or colour variations but are two character jugs which have undergone a full production run. Their high market values however mean they must be classified as rarities even though both are fairly easily obtained on the discontinued market.
Red Hair Clown — Large — Produced 1937-42
Market Value   £1500-£2000 $5500-$6000
White Hair Clown — Large — Produced 1951-55
Market Value   £600-£900 $1100-$1300
Brown Hair Clown
This jug is a variation of the red hair clown which has only been confirmed as existing. Bearing the same registration number as the red hair version D5610 it has brown coloured hair and slightly different facial markings and colourings.

The Cabinetmaker
Intended as part of the Williamsburg series, this large size character jug was announced in 1981 but never released on to the market. Several were made and are stored in the Royal Doulton Factory. So far none have escaped from the Factory on to the Doulton market so their value is impossible to determine.

Ears Up Anne of Cleves
First introduced in 1980 and still produced today. The large Anne of Cleves has a horses head on its handle. The first models produced had the horses ears sticking upright out of the body. This was changed soon after, the ears lying flat as there was a difficulty in packing the original jug. The early version is now highly sought after and has been accordingly rapidly rising in value.
Market Value: £250-£300 $350-$450

Single Rat Pied Piper Handle
Two examples of the Pied Piper with one large rat on the handle as compared to the three usually found have been reported. Again these are probably early trial pieces.

Small & Miniature Yachtsman
These pilots are now confirmed as existing. An example of both turned up in the Midlands in 1984 and reportedly sold for over £1000 ($1400) each.

The Toothless Granny alongside the normal Granny.

The Goatee Beard Cavalier alongside the normal Cavalier.

Goatee Beard — Cavalier
This is another early version which went through a mould change, although in this case it was only minor. This version has a distinctive goatee beard as opposed to the bare chin of later models. Originally thought to have only been made in the large size, a small size has been reported to exist. I have not yet seen this jug so cannot confirm its existence. It would of course be highly valuable.
Large: £1000-£1400 $4000-$5000

Toothless — Granny
Not considered to be as rare as either of previous mould variations, this jug is identifiable by its lack of a prominent front tooth. (It is reported to almost always carry an 'A' mark). There are other slight variations with the normal Granny, particularly in their hairlines. Recorded as only being produced in the large size there are persistent rumours of it existing in a small size. It is my opinion that it does not exist in the small size and that suspect slight differences in painting are responsible for such rumours.
Market Value: £800-£1000 $1200-$1400

Miniature Old Salt
The character 'Old Salt' was introduced as a large and small size character jug in 1961 and is still produced today. In 1983 it was introduced in the miniature size with a small handle change, (there is no longer a space in the crook of the mermaids arm). At least 100 exist with the original handle, presumably pilots made before the design changed. These pilots after a slightly strange start are now climbing rapidly in value.
Market Value: £400 plus $700 plus

Yellow Crown Old King Cole Musical Jug
Two examples of this have turned up in the last year. One was discovered in South Africa and the other in England. These are far too rare to place a value on.

Yellow Crown — Old King Cole
An early version of the 'Old King Cole' jug, this version has a yellow crown as opposed to the more common orange. It also has other variations as both versions were made from completely different moulds. The 'yellow crown' was made in both large and small sizes, the small size being the rarer of the two. The

jug is known to exist without mould variations in both sizes. Due to its rarity the market values given are tentative.

Large: £900-£1000 $2000-$3000
Small: £1000-£1200 $2500-$3500

Clark Gable

This jug was initially produced for the current celebrity series in 1984. For some reason the first shipment of these jugs to the USA was recalled; however at least 60 of these jugs had been sold to the public. All the jugs recalled were subsequently destroyed and plans to produce the model were dropped. It is rumoured this was due to Clark Gable's estate not approving the likeness. Royal Doulton declined to comment on this rumour. The jug has subsequently shot up in value, as there is no doubt that the jug now holds a pilot rarity rating.

Market Value: £2500-£3000 $3000-$4000

Hatless Drake

The existence of this jug was only confirmed in 1981, yet since then a surprising number have appeared. At least six were available at one of the 1984 specialist Doulton fairs. Originally thought to another mould variation, it must have in fact been an early version of the 'Drake' character jug. It only exists in the large size and a colour variation with a green instead of red jacket is known.

Market Value: £2700-£3300 $5000-$6000

Clark Gable, Hatless Drake, Mr Quaker

Mr Quaker

Whilst not as rare as the other jugs in this section, this jug does deserve to be listed as a rarity. Issued this year, the jug has a very unusual background. It is a Limited Edition of 3500 produced to commemorate the 85th anniversary of Quaker Oats Ltd., established in London, England in 1899. Of the 3500 jugs made, 1100 were made available to North American collectors for over $100 each and slightly less than 200 were made available to British collectors selling at £30 each. The remainer are being used by Quaker Oats Ltd., as promotional gifts to selected customers and suppliers. These have apparently been well received and therefore one would expect only a few to appear on the market. This makes Mr Quaker the smallest limited edition of a large character jug produced with only 1300 available to collectors.

    The jug itself is based on the portrait of Mr Quaker by the illustrator Haddon Sunblom and is designed by Harry Salts of Royal Doulton. As can be seen from the photograph above the combination of colours used and the fine details incorporated in the design produce a very attractive character jug indeed — partly, no doubt, due to the man whose idea led to the jug being produced, George J. Yapp, the Managing Director of Quaker Oats and an avid collector of large jugs. George describes the experience as a particular thrill for him as a collector to be involved in the development of a character jug. This apparently took several months and many modifications to the design were required before a satisfactory character jug was produced.

It is far too early to place a value on this jug for at the time of writing it has only just been released. I expect this jug to be massively over subscribed, with those who obtain it unlikely to resell it. Its eventual market value will, I am sure, be very high indeed.

Small Tam O'Shanter Colour Variation
This version has a distinct blue coloured hat which is heavily ridged as compared to the smooth surface on the normal version. Other differences are noticable in the jug's finer details and colouring with a stronger brown and green used for both the jug and doll depicted on the handle. To date only one example bearing an early backstamp has been reported. It is certainly a trial example produced as a forerunner to the normal version.

White Churchill
Not really a character jug, although regarded as one by collectors. It is a loving cup with two handles, produced between 1940-41. This extremely rare jug has an inscription on its base which reads "Winston Spencer Churchill Prime Minister 1940. This loving cup was made during the 'Battle of Britain' as a tribute to a great leader". Two coloured versions of this jug are known to exist, one of which is restored. These coloured jugs do not carry an inscription. Differing slightly in colouring shades, they have blue shoulders and bow ties with coloured hair and a pale complexion. It is impossible to place a market value to the only two colour versions of this variation known.
White
Churchill: £4000-£6000 $8000-$10000

Rumoured Pilots
All of these jugs are rumoured to exist from reliable sources, but no actual proof has been shown to the author — if they do exist and were to appear on the market, they would be expected to fetch a very high price.
Small Golfer
Miniature Golfer
Miniature Paddy D6151
Large Williamsburg Colour Variations

Gold Handled Beefeater
This large GR version Beefeater is a colour variation. The back of its handle has a very distinctive gold thread elaboration to it, which distinguishes it from the ordinary beefeater. A highly sought after jug, its value has been rising rapidly recently.
Market Value: £1000-£2000 $2000-$3000

McCallum
A large size jug made in the mid-thirties to early forties for D. M. McCallum Whisky Distillers. It depicts a typical Highlander Scot and three variations are known to exist. Other manufacturers of the period particularly Wade produced identical jugs (excepting the backstamp) which are of minor value compared to Doulton versions.

Kingsware McCallum
Produced in the distinctive brown Kingsware Glaze this jug is highly sought after by collectors. A very rare jug which is highly valued on the Doulton markets.
Market Value   £1500-£2000 $2500-$3500

The White McCallum
Identical to the Kingsware version except for its lack of colouring and different glazing, this jug is the more common of the two. It is nearly always crazed on the outside.
Market Value   £700-£1000 $1100-$1400

A white McCallum. (Courtesy Dick Nicholson)

A large Arry with a small blue Pearly Boy, a miniature brown and white Pearly Boy and the tiny Arry. (Courtesy Tom Power)

The Pearly Boy and Pearly Girl

These are a variation of the 'Arry and 'Arriet and represent the traditional cockney Pearly Kings & Queens. The Pearly Boy is identifiable by the 'pearls' or 'buttons' running down his head, side of the jug and around the collar. There are several colour variations amongst the pearly boys and all are considered very rare. The three versions are brown, brown and white, and blue. Blue being the rarest.

Pearly Boy:	Brown		Blue	
Large:	£500-£800	$850-$950	£2000-£2500	$3500-$4500
Small:	£400-£500	$550-$650	£1400-£1600	$3000-$3500
Miniature:	£250-£300	$400-$500	£1400-£1600	$3000-$3500

Pearly girls have no additional buttons and except for the colouring are identical to the 'Arriet jug. It has a bright lime green handle and hatfeather. The hat brim is red/maroon, as is the large button as the base of the feather. The hair is very dark brown, and the scarf is bright red. The pearly girls are far rarer than the pearly boys, and although particularly valuable it is difficult to put an exact value on them.

Miniature Trapper
A surprising number of pilot versions have turned up in the last year of this jug, particularly in the UK. There must have been several sample pieces produced before the character was withdrawn in all sizes.
Market Value: £1300-£1500 $1800-$2000

Miniature Lumberjack
Produced and withdrawn in the same year as the Trapper jugs. The Lumberjack jugs also have miniature pilot versions occasionally turning up. Their existence and story is identical to that of the miniature Trapper and it is judged to be of comparable value.
Market Value: £1300-£1500 $1800-$2000

Half Size Jockey
Two versions of this are reported to exist, both of which although not carrying the Doulton Back Stamp have been confirmed as Doulton by the International Collectors Club. The example photographed in this book is in the hands of a private collector in Sheffield.

Baseball Player, Buffalo Bill, Maori
These three large jugs are all pilot jugs. For one reason or another Royal Doulton after producing the designed jug in its pilot form decided not to commercially produce the jug. One Baseball Player is known to exist in the Royal Doulton Museum and one example of Buffalo Bill is in a private US collection. Two versions of the Maori were produced and it is rumoured that more than one example of each exists. As none of these jugs have appeared on the market their value cannot be estimated.

The miniature pilot Trapper and Lumberjack.

The pilot Baseball Player. (Courtesy RDICC)

The half size Jockey alongside the normal version.

'Toby Gillette' Character Jug

This character jug, of which only three exist , has a most unusual background story. It was created through a programme on B.B.C. Television in the U.K. called "Jim'll Fix It" presented by Jimmy Saville O.B.E. Viewers, mainly children, write in to the programme asking that their dearest wishes and dreams may be fulfilled. Jim and his staff make sure that no matter how weird the request e.g. riding a horse in a circus or ordering sausage and marmalade sandwiches at the Ritz Hotel, it actually takes place.

In early 1984, a little boy of twelve named Toby Gillette wrote to Jimmy Saville asking if he could have a Toby jug made of himself. With the co-operation of Royal Doulton three Character jugs were made of Toby Gillette because it was felt that Toby jugs were unsuitable for portraying young people. The making of this jug and Toby Gillette's tour round the Royal Doulton factory were later shown on the "Jim'll Fix It" programme.

Of the three jugs made, one was presented to Toby Gillette, one was kept for Royal Doulton's own collection and the third was given by Jimmy Saville to be auctioned for charity. The presence of what can only be decribed as a 'pilot' jug aroused world wide interest in Doulton collectors. Prior to the auction, speculation among dealers and collectors in London as to the price it would bring ranged from £4000-£10,000. The auctioneers, Sotheby's of London, had placed an estimate of £400-£800 on this jug. At the eventual auction, recorded under the glare of B.B.C. cameras, the bidding was brisk. The auctioneer's own estimate was rapidly passed. Several bidders in at the start retired once the price had reached ten thousand pounds. Eventually, the bidding was between a South African collector and an American Royal Doulton dealer, Barry Weiss, who paid £14500 plus commission for the jug. This bid currently holds the record for the highest price paid for a Royal Doulton jug at auction or by private sale.

One wonders what sum the only other example which could conceivably come on the market, Toby Gillette's own jug, would now fetch. I should imagine it would sell at an even higher price making Toby a very fortunate little boy indeed.

As a result of the price reached, I would expect other rare 'pilot' jugs e.g. Buffalo Bill, Maori and The Baseball Player to fetch a similar price if they were also to appear in an auction, although as in all rare Royal Doulton items, who knows?

26

Buying Discontinued Character Jugs

For any new collector of character jugs, here is a list of buying tips to help you to build up your collection. Certain sections should also be of interest to existing collectors.

1) When buying from antique fairs or a market, it is best to get there as early as possible because jugs that are rare or cheap are always sold early on, usually to the trade.

2) Be prepared to travel when searching for jugs as there are differences in both price and availability in different parts of the country.

3) Shop around whenever possible as prices vary considerably between dealers, even in the same antique fair or market.

4) Try to visit junk shops and jumble sales as occasionally jugs turn up in these places selling at a fraction of their true value.

5) Always examine jugs carefully under a strong light to detect hairline cracks or a restoration. In addition to this, ask a dealer to guarantee that the jug you are buying is perfect.

6) Get to know individual Doulton Dealers. They will keep you in touch with developments in the Doulton market and could result in you obtaining pieces at favourable prices.

7) To obtain rarer jugs, try placing orders with individual dealers. A large proportion of pieces never appear on the open market but are sold directly to the collector who has previously placed an order with the dealer.

8) Contact auction houses in your area regularly to inquire if they have any jugs in forthcoming sales. It is relatively easy to leave bids if you can't attend the auction yourself.

9) Try to meet the collectors. This will be useful for buying or swapping jugs and you will derive even greater pleasure from making new friends as you do so.

10) The market value of discontinued jugs can rise or fall, so try to keep well informed. I suggest collectors note the prices they hear or see to ensure that they always buy in line with market prices.

11) Subscribe to the International Royal Doulton Collectors' Club. This organisation costs very little to join and provides several benefits to members who are issued with a three-monthly illustrated magazine with all the latest news on the Doulton world. The Collectors' Club Gallery at Leather and Snook, 167 Piccadilly, London, displays regularly changing exhibits of Doulton wares. For details and an application form, contact any of the following branches:

UK Headquarters
  Royal Doulton
  International Collectors Club
  5 Egmont House
  116 Shaftesbury Avenue
  London W1V 7DE.

USA Branch
  Doulton & Co Inc
  PO Box 1815
  Somerset
  NJ 08873

Canadian Branch
  Doulton Canada Inc
  850 Progress Avenue
  Scarborough
  Ontario MIH 3C4

Australian Branch
  Doulton Tableware Pty Ltd
  Inc NSW
  PO Box 47
  17-23 Merriwa Street
  Gordon
  NSW 2072

12) **Recommended UK Antique Fairs**
All antique fairs are worth visiting as many antique dealers carry the old Doulton items. Those listed below are regularly attended by the author and usually have a few Doulton Specialist dealers displaying Doulton jugs.

See Exchange & Mart for details

Queens Hall — Leeds

Bingly Hall — Stafford

Birmingham

Alexandra Palace — London (500 stalls; 1985 dates: 19th May-14th July/7th & 20th October)

Doncaster Racecourse — Yorkshire

Royal Horticultural — London

13) **Recommended Antique Markets**
Portobello Road, London
The London centre for Doulton dealing. There are four major Doulton dealers in Portobello Road and numerous other dealers who always have pieces of Doulton for sale. Notting Hill Gate is the nearest Tube station to the market which is held every Saturday.

Camden Passage, London*Tube: Angel* Every Wednesday

Charnock Richard, Lancs *off the M6* every Sunday

14 **The Doulton Fairs**
There are now 4 Doulton Fairs held every year. Three in the USA and one in England. Each fair is comprised solely of Doulton dealers with the DCC also usually exhibiting.

   The UK Fair in October 1984proved a roaring success. Twenty dealers from all over the UK plus one from the USA displayed one of the best ranges of Doulton seen in the UK.

15) **UK Auctioneers**
All auction houses commonly sell Doulton along with other collections and antiques. The auction houses listed below all either hold special Doulton sales or regularly feature Doulton in general sales.

US auctioneers will be listed in the next issue.

Peter Wilson & Co,
Market Street
Nanwich, Cheshire
CW5 5DG
Tel: 0270 623878
contact Miss R Woodward

Abridge Auctions,
Market Place,
Abridge, Essex
Tel: 8492107
contact Mick Yewman

Louis Taylors,
Percy Street,
Morley, Stoke on Trent
Tel: 0782 260222

Phillips,
7 Blenheim Street,
London W1
Tel: 01 584 9161 *contact* Keith Baker

Christies South Kensington,
85 Old Brompton Road,
London SW5 3JS
Tel: 01 581 2231 *contact* Paul Bathaud

Sotheby's
34-35 New Bond Street
London W1A 2AA
Tel: 01 443 8080 *contact* Michael Turner

16 **Selected UK Current Doulton Retailers**
London — Leather & Snook 167 Piccadilly, W1 Tel: 01-493 9121
Manchester — T Hayward & Sons 62/66 Deansgate
Durham — Home & Leisure Centre, Milburngate Shopping Centre
Belfast — R Hogg & Co, 10 Danegall Square West
Glasgow — Trevons, 254 Sauchieshall Street
Edinburgh — Les Cadeaux, 121 Rose Street
York — Mulberry Hall, Stonegate
Leeds — Lewis's, The Headrow
Swansea — David Evans, Princess Way
Rowtenstall — My Fair Lady, 4 Bacup Road

17 **Character Jug Collectors Clubs**
Both of these are well worth joining!
The Character Jug Chapter
Box 5000, Caldeon,
Ontario, LON ICO
Canada
Annual Subscription Can$9 Canada (Can$12 outside Canada)

The Jug Collector
PO Box 91748,
Long Beach,
California 90809
Annual Subscription US$3 USA (US$6 outside USA)

Alphabetical Listing of Discontinued Character Jugs

Character	Production Dates	Large	Small	Available in Miniature	Tiny	Intermediate
'Ard of Earing	1964-67	□	□	□	□	■
'Arriet	1947-60	□	□	□	□	■
'Arry	1947-60	□	□	□	□	■
Apothecary	1963-83	□	□	□	■	■
Auld Mac (Owd version)	1938-45	□	□	■	□	■
Beafeater (GR Handle)	1947-53	□	□	□	■	■
Bootmaker	1963-83	□	□	□	□	■
Blacksmith	1963-83	□	□	□	□	■
Buz Fuz	1948-60	■	□	■	■	□
Captain Ahab	1959-84	□	□	□	■	■
Captain Cuttle	1948-60	■	□	■	■	□
Captain Henry Morgan	1958-81	□	□	□	■	■
Captain Hook	1965-71	□	□	□	■	■
Captain Ahab	1959-84	□	□	□	■	■
Cardinal	1936-60	□	□	□	□	■
Cavalier	1940-60	□	□	■	■	■
Cavalier (goatee beard version)	1940	□	■	■	■	■
Churchill	1940-42	□	■	■	■	■
Clown Red hair	1937-42	□	■	■	■	■
Clown White hair	1951-55	□	■	■	■	■
Custer & Sitting Bull	1984	□	■	■	■	■
Dick Turpin (1st version)	1935-60	□	□	□	■	■
Dick Turpin (2nd version)	1960-80	□	□	□	■	■
Dick Whittington	1953-60	□	■	■	■	■
Drake	1940-60	□	□	■	■	■
Drake (hatless version)	1940	□	■	■	■	■
Farmer John	1938-60	■	□	■	■	■
Fat Boy	1940-60	■	□	□	□	□
Fortune Teller	1954-67	□	□	□	■	■
Friar Tuck	1951-60	□	■	■	■	■
Gardener	1973-80	□	□	□	■	■
Gladiator	1961-67	□	□	□	■	■
Gondolier	1964-69	□	□	□	■	■
Gaoler	1963-83	□	□	□	■	■
Gone Away	1960-81	□	□	□	■	■
Granny	1935-84	□	□	□	■	■
Grant & Lee	1983	□	■	■	■	■
Guardsman	1963-83	□	□	□	■	■
Gunsmith	1963-83	□	□	□	■	■
Gulliver	1962-67	□	□	□	■	■
Izaac Walton	1952-82	□	□	■	■	■
Jarge	1950-60	□	□	■	■	■
Jester	1936-60	■	□	■	■	■
Jockey	1971-75	□	■	■	■	■
John Barleycorn	1934-60	□	□	□	■	■
John Doulton	1984	■	□	■	■	■
John Peel	1936-60	□	□	□	□	■
Johnny Appleseed	1953-69	□	■	■	■	■
Lord Nelson	1952-69	□	■	■	■	■
Lumberjack	1967-82	□	□	P	■	■
Mae West (American Express Edition)	1982	□	■	■	■	■

Character	Production Dates	Large	Small	Miniature	Tiny	Intermediate
Mad Hatter	1965-83	□	□	□	■	■
Mephistopheles	1937-48	□	□	■	■	■
Mikado	1959-69	□	□	□	■	■
Mine Host	1958-81	□	□	□	■	■
Monty (colour change)	1946-54	□	■	■	■	■
Mr Micawber	1940-60	■	□	□	□	□
Mr Pickwick	1940-60	□	□	□	□	□
Mr Quaker	1985	□	■	■	■	■
Night Watchman	1963-83	□	□	□	■	■
Old Charley	1934-83	□	□	□	□	■
Old King Cole	1939-60	□	□	■	■	■
Old King Cole (yellow version)	1937	□	□	■	■	■
Paddy	1937-60	□	□	□	□	■
Parson Brown	1935-60	□	□	■	■	■
Pearly Boy Brown	1947	□	□	□	□	■
Pearly Boy Blue	1947	□	□	□	□	■
Pearly Girl Brown	1947	□	□	□	□	■
Pearly Girl Blue	1947	□	□	□	□	■
Pied Piper	1954-80	□	□	□	□	■
Punch & Judy Man	1964-69	□	□	□	□	■
Regency Beau	1962-67	□	□	□	□	■
Robin Hood (1st version)	1947-60	□	□	□	□	■
Robinson Crusoe	1960-82	□	□	□	□	■
Sairey Gamp	1940-60	(In current production)			□	■
Samuel Johnson	1950-60	□	□	■	■	■
Sam Weller	1940-60	□	□	□	□	□
Sancho Panza	1957-82	□	□	□	■	■
Santa Claus						
(1981 version Doll Handle)		□	■	■	■	■
(1982 version Reindeer Handle)		□	■	■	■	■
(1983 version Sack of Toys Handle)		□	■	■	■	■
Scaramouche	1962-67	□	□	□	■	■
Simple Simon	1953-60	□	■	■	■	■
Simon the Cellarer	1935-60	□	□	■	■	■
Smuggler	1968-80	□	□	■	■	■
Smuts	1946-48	□	■	■	■	■
St. George	1968-75	□	□	■	■	■
Tam O'Shanter	1973-79	□	□	□	□	■
Toby Philpots	1937-69	□	□	□	□	■
Tony Weller*	1936-60	□	□	□	□	■
Toothless Granny	1935	□	■	■	■	■
Touchstone	1936-60	□	■	■	■	■
Town Crier	1960-73	□	□	□	□	■
Trapper	1967-82	□	□	P	■	■
Ugly Duchess	1965-73	□	□	□	■	■
Uncle Tom Cobbleigh	1952-60	□	■	■	■	■
Vicar of Bray	1936-60	□	■	■	■	■
Viking	1959-75	□	□	□	■	■
Veteran Motorist	1973-83	□	□	□	□	■
Walrus & Carpenter	1965-79	□	□	□	□	■
Yachtsman	1971-79	□	P	P	■	■

* Extra large version also available
□ Sizes available
■ Sizes not available
P Pilot issued

Alphabetical Listing of In-Production Character Jugs

Character	Year of Introduction	Large	Small	Miniature	Medium
				Available in	
Annie Oakley	1985	■	■	■	□
Anthony & Cleopatra	1985	□	■	■	■
Anne Boleyn	1975	□	■	■	■
Anne of Cleves	1980	□	■	■	■
Aramis	1956	□	□	□	■
Athos	1956	□	□	□	■
Auld Mac	1938	□	□	□	■
Bacchus	1959	□	□	□	■
Beefeater	1947	□	□	□	■
Benjamin Franklin	1983	■	□	■	■
Buffalo Bill	1985	■	■	■	□
Catherine of Aragon	1975	□	■	□	■
Catherine Howard	1978	□	■	■	■
Catherine Parr	1981	□	■	■	■
Davy Crockett & Santa Anna	1985	□	■	■	■
D'Artagnan	1983	□	■	□	■
Don Quixote	1957	□	■	□	■
Doc Holliday	1985	■	■	■	□
Elvis Presley	1985	□	■	■	■
The Fireman	1984	□	□	□	■
Falstaff	1950	□	□	□	■
Falconer	1960	□	■	□	■
George Washington	1982	□	■	■	■
Golfer	1971	□	■	■	■
George Harrison	1984	■	■	■	□
Geronimo	1985	■	■	■	□
Groucho Marx	1984	□	■	■	■
Hamlet	1982	□	■	■	■
Henry V	1982	□	■	■	■
Henry VIII	1975	□	□	□	■
Humphrey Bogart	1985	□	■	■	■
Jane Seymour	1979	□	■	■	■
Jimmy Durante (to be withdrawn in 1985)	1984	□	■	■	■
John Lennon	1984	■	■	■	□
Lawyer	1959	□	□	□	■
Long John Silver	1952	□	□	□	■
Louis Armstrong	1984	□	■	■	■
Lobster Man	1968	□	□	□	■
Monty	1946	□	□	□	■
Macbeth	1982	□	■	■	■
Mae West	1982	□	■	■	■
Mark Twain	1980	□	□	■	■
Merlin	1960	□	□	□	■
North American Indian	1967	□	□	□	■
Neptune	1961	□	□	□	■
Old Salt	1961	□	□	□	■
Othello	1982	□	■	■	■
Paul McCartney	1984	■	■	■	□
Porthos	1956	□	□	□	■
Poacher	1955	□	□	□	■
Ronald Reagan	1984	□	■	■	■
Romeo	1983	□	■	■	■
Ringo Starr	1984	■	■	■	□
Robin Hood (2nd version)	1960	□	□	□	■
Rip Van Winkle	1955	□	□	□	■
Sairey Gamp	1935	□	□	□	■
Sleuth	1973	□	□	□	■
Santa Claus	1984	□	□	□	■
William Shakespeare	1983	□	■	■	■
Wild Bill Hickock	1985	■	■	■	□
Wyatt Earp	1985	■	■	■	□

□ Sizes available   ■ Sizes not available

Discontinued Character Jug Market Values

In this book the market value of each discontinued figure jug is given in the form of a price range. This reflects the Doulton market where prices are know to vary around the margin on individual pieces. The very circumstances of a particular purchase may influence its price, for example, a dealer may intentionally price an item higher becuase he deems the collector demand in his area to be sufficient to warrant a higher sum. Another dealer could price the same item below market value in order to ensure a quick sale. The particular need for a jug may also influence its price. A collector requiring only one more piece to complete a set will place a higher value on this piece than on any of the set he already has. The result of these marginal differences in value between both collectors and dealers is that there is no fixed market price for any Doulton item. However, by collating a number of individual prices for each item it is possible to estimate the market price range. The prices given in this book are based on prices observed and collected by the author over a three monthly period prior to publication. The Doulton market changes rapidly with market values rising and falling, so always attempt to check values given with current market prices to identify changes in the market values listed in this section.

Character Jug Sizes (approx)

Tiny	1¼ inches	Intermediate	5 inches
Miniature	2½ inches	Large	7 inches
Small	4 inches	Extra Large	8 inches
Medium (New Size)	5½ inches		

The 1960's group of withdrawals, which have all been rising rapidly in the last few years.

Anne of Cleves (Ears Up) (Designer M. Abberley)

The fourth wife of Henry VIII

Size	D. Number	Production Dates	£	$	Date Acquired	Price Paid	
Large	6653	1980-	£200-£300	$300-$400	_____	_____	☐

'Ard of 'Earing (Designer D. Biggs)

Depicts an English phrase made popular in the 1920's

Size	D. Number	Production Dates	£	$	Date Acquired	Price Paid	
Large	6588	1964-67	£400-£650	$1000-$1500	_____	_____	☐
Small	6591	1964-67	£400-£500	$650-$750	_____	_____	☐
Miniature	6594	1964-67	£700-£900	$1200-$1300	_____	_____	☐

'Arriet (Designer H. Fenton)

Depicts a London cockney costermonger. Early versions of this jug prior to 1951 have distinctive blonde hair

Size	D. Number	Production Dates	£	$	Date Acquired	Price Paid	
Large	6208	1947-60	£110-£130	$175-$200	_____	_____	☐
Small	6236	1947-60	£50-£60	$90-$100	_____	_____	☐
Miniature	6250	1947-60	£40-£50	$80-$90	_____	_____	☐
Tiny	6256	1947-60	£80-£90	$200-$225	_____	_____	☐

'Arry (Designer H. Fenton)

Another London cockney costermonger, designed as 'Arriet's companion. Pre 1951 versions have a different shade of yellow on their scarf

Size	D. Number	Production Dates	£	$	Date Acquired	Price Paid	
Large	6207	1947-60	£110-£130	$175-$200	_____	_____	☐
Small	6235	1947-60	£45-£60	$90-$100	_____	_____	☐
Miniature	6249	1947-60	£40-£50	$80-$90	_____	_____	☐
Tiny	6255	1947-60	£80-£90	$200-$225	_____	_____	☐

Apothecary (Designer M. Henk)

From the character jugs of Williamsburg series depicting American colonial life

Size	D. Number	Production Dates	£	$	Date Acquired	Price Paid	
Large	6567	1963-83	£30-£45	$50-$60	_____	_____	☐
Small	6574	1963-83	£18-£25	$35-$45	_____	_____	☐
Miniature	6581	1963-83	£16-£20	$25-$35	_____	_____	☐

Auld Mac/Owd Mac (Designer H. Fenton)

A miserly Scotsman. Early versions of this jug have brown green shoulders as opposed to light green

Size	D. Number	Production Dates	£	$	Date Acquired	Price Paid	
Large Owd Mac	5823	1938-45	£40-£45	$65-$75	_____	_____	☐
Small Owd Mac	5824	1938-45	£20-£25	$45-$55	_____	_____	☐
Tiny Auld Mac	6257	1946-60	£110-£130	$225-$250	_____	_____	☐

Beefeater (GR Handle Version) (Designer H. Fenton)

A member of the Yeoman of the Guard — current models have ER on the handle

Large	6206	1947-53	£45-£60	$110-$120	_____	_____	☐
Small	6233	1947-53	£25-£30	$60-$70	_____	_____	☐
Miniature	6251	1947-53	£25-£30	$60-$70	_____	_____	☐
Large Gold Handle		1947-	£1700-£2000	$3000-$3500	_____	_____	☐

Bootmaker (Designer D. Briggs)

A Williamsburg Series character

Large	6572	1963-83	£30-£45	$50-$60	_____	_____	☐
Small	6579	1963-83	£18-£25	$35-$40	_____	_____	☐
Miniature	6586	1963-83	£16-£20	$30-$35	_____	_____	☐

Blacksmith (Designer D. Briggs)

A Williamsburg Series character

Large	6571	1963-83	£30-£35	$50-$60	_____	_____	☐
Small	6578	1963-83	£18-£22	$35-$40	_____	_____	☐
Miniature	6585	1963-83	£16-£20	$30-$35	_____	_____	☐

Buz Fuz (Designers L. Harradine & H. Fenton)

The Barrister in Charles Dickens' novel, 'Dombey and Son'

Intermediate	5838	1938-48	£90-£110	$190-$200	_____	_____	☐
Small	5838	1948-60	£55-£65	$100-$110	_____	_____	☐
PickKwick advertising Jug. Limited edition of 2000							
Small		1982	£60-£70	$100-$120	_____	_____	☐

Captain Ahab (Designer G. Sharp)

The captain in the Moby Dick story

Large	6500	1959-84	£30-£35	$60-$70	_____	_____	☐
Small	6506	1959-84	£15-£20	$30-$40	_____	_____	☐
Miniature	6522	1959-84	£13-£18	$25-$35	_____	_____	☐

Captain Henry Morgan (Designer G. Sharp)

A famous 17th century British buccaneer

Large	6467	1958-81	£35-£45	$70-$80	_____	_____	☐
Small	6469	1958-81	£20-£25	$40-$50	_____	_____	☐
Miniature	6510	1960-81	£18-£23	$35-$40	_____	_____	☐

Captain Hook (Designers M. Henk & D. Biggs)
A pirate Captain in the book, 'Peter Pan'

Large	6597	1965-71	£275-£325	$400-$500	____ ____	☐
Small	6601	1965-71	£230-£260	$325-$375	____ ____	☐
Miniature	6605	1965-71	£230-£260	$350-$400	____ ____	☐

Captain Cuttle (Designers L. Harradine & H. Fenton)
A character from Dickens' Dombey and Son

Intermediate	5842	1938-48	£85-£95	$180-$200	____ ____	☐
Small	5842	1938-48	£55-£65	$100-$110	____ ____	☐

Cardinal (Designer C. J. Noke)
Possibly representing Cardinal Wolsey from the reign of Henry VIII

Large	5614	1936-60	£65-£75	$140-160	____ ____	☐
Small	6033	1939-60	£40-£45	$80-$90	____ ____	☐
Miniature	6129	1940-60	£32-£38	$60-$70	____ ____	☐
Tiny	6258	1947-60	£110-£120	$225-$250	____ ____	☐

Cavalier (Designer H. Fenton)
A name given to the supporters of Charles 1st during the English Civil War. Early versions prior to 1950 have a different shade of green on their hat

Large	6114	1940-60	£65-£75	$130-$150	____ ____	☐
Small	6173	1941-60	£40-£45	$70-$80	____ ____	☐
Large Goatee	6114	1940-42	£1000-£1400	$4000-$5000	____ ____	☐

Churchill (Designer C. J. Noke)
Prime Minister of Great Britain during World War Two

Large	6170	1940	£5000-£6000	$8000-$10000	____ ____	☐

Clark Gable (Designer Stan Taylor)
A film star from the Celebrity Collection

Large	6709	1984	£3000-£4000	$4000-$6000	____ ____	☐

Clown (Designer H. Fenton)
A comic character from the circus

Large (Red hair)	5610	1937-42	£1500-£2000	$5000-$5500	____ ____	☐
Large (Brown hair)	5610	1937-42	£2000-£2500	$5500-$6000	____ ____	☐
Large (White hair)	6322	1951-55	£600-£900	$1100-$1300	____ ____	☐

Dick Turpin (First Version) (Designers C. J. Noke & H. Fenton)
A notorious English eighteenth century highway man

Large	5485	1935-60	£65-£75	$140-$150			☐
Small	5618	1936-60	£35-£40	$70-$80			☐
Miniature	6128	1940-60	£28-£35	$50-$60			☐

Dick Turpin (Second Version) (Designer D. Biggs)
This version has a mask and a horse shaped handle

Large	6528	1960-80	£35-£45	$60-$70			☐
Small	5635	1960-80	£20-£25	$45-$55			☐
Miniature	6542	1960-80	£14-£18	$35-$40			☐

Dick Whittington (Designer M. Henk)
A 15th Century Lord Mayor of London

Large	6375	1953-60	£220-£260	$350-$400			☐

Drake (Designer H. Fenton)
The famous British sea captain, Sir Francis Drake (1545-96)

Large	6115	1940-60	£65-£75	$145-$155			☐
Small	6174	1941-60	£35-£45	$75-$85			☐
Large Hatless		1940-41	£3000-£3500	$5000-$6000			☐

Farmer John (Designer C. J. Noke)
Depicts the traditional English farmer, early version has the handle entering the top of the jug and is worth slightly more

Large	5788	1938-60	£65-£80	$140-$170			☐
Small	5789	1938-60	£45-£55	$80-$100			☐

Fat Boy (Designers L. Harradine & H. Fenton)
Another Charles Dickens character from the Pickwick Papers

Intermediate	5840	1938-48	£85-£95	$180-$200			☐
Small	5840	1948-60	£45-£55	$100-$120			☐
Miniature	6139	1940-60	£35-£45	$70-$80			☐
Tiny	6142	1940-60	£55-£65	$130-$140			☐

Fortune Teller (Designer G. Sharp)
Depicts a traditional Romany character

Large	6497	1959-67	£260-£300	$475-$500			☐
Small	6503	1959-67	£220-£260	$360-$390			☐
Miniature	6523	1960-67	£220-£260	$400-$450			☐

Friar Tuck (Designer H. Fenton)

A character from the Robin Hood legend

Large	6321	1951-60	£230-£280	$375-$400	_____	_____	☐

Granny (Designers M. Fenton and M. Henk)

Depicts a traditional old Granny

Large	5521	1935-83	£35-£40	$70-$80	_____	_____	☐
Small	6384	1935-83	£20-£25	$50-$60	_____	_____	☐
Miniature	6220	1935-83	£15-£20	$40-$50	_____	_____	☐

Granny (Toothless Version) (Designers H. Fenton & M. Henk)

A early mould variation of the Granny

Large	5521	1935	£800-£1000	$1300-$1500	_____	_____	☐

Gardener (Designer D. Biggs)

Depicts a knowledgable British gardener

Large	6630	1973-80	£35-£50	$90-$100	_____	_____	☐
Small	6634	1973-80	£25-£30	$50-$60	_____	_____	☐
Miniature	6638	1973-80	£20-£25	$35-$45	_____	_____	☐

George Armstrong Custer and Sitting Bull

(Designer M. Abberley)
The second in The Antagonists series. A limited edition of 9500 now sold out. Two opposing figures from American Western history. There are two versions of this jug identical but for the colour of Sitting Bull's eyes, one version's are brown while the other is grey-blue.

Large		1984	£65-£75	$100-$120	_____	_____	☐

Gladiator (Designer M. Henk)

A professional fighter from the days of the Roman Empire

Large	6550	1961-67	£320-£360	$475-$525	_____	_____	☐
Small	6553	1961-67	£240-£300	$375-$400	_____	_____	☐
Miniature	6556	1961-67	£220-£260	$400-$425	_____	_____	☐

Gondolier (Designer D. Biggs)

Depicts one of the singing boat-men of Venice

Large	6589	1964-69	£260-£320	$550-$600	_____	_____	☐
Small	6592	1964-69	£220-£250	$375-$400	_____	_____	☐
Miniature	6595	1964-69	£240-£270	$425-$450	_____	_____	☐

Gaoler (Designer D. Biggs)

Another Williamsburg Series Character

Large	6570	1963-83	£30-£45	$50-$60	_____	_____	☐
Small	6577	1963-83	£18-£25	$30-$40	_____	_____	☐
Miniature	6584	1963-83	£16-£20	$30-$40	_____	_____	☐

Gone Away (Designer G. Sharp)

Depicts a traditional British huntsman

Large	6531	1960-81	£35-£40	$60-$70	_____	_____	☐
Small	6538	1960-81	£20-£25	$35-$45	_____	_____	☐
Miniature	6545	1960-81	£15-£20	$35-$45	_____	_____	☐

Grant and Lee (Designer M. Abberley)

Two opposing Generals from the American Civil War.

Large	6698	1983	£85-£95	$120-$140	_____	_____	☐

Guardsman (Designer M. Henk)

A character from the Williamsburg Series

Large	6568	1963-83	£30-£40	$50-$60	_____	_____	☐
Small	6575	1963-83	£20-£25	$35-$45	_____	_____	☐
Miniature	6582	1963-83	£15-£20	$30-$40	_____	_____	☐

Gunsmith (Designer D. Biggs)

A character from the Williamsburg Series

Large	6573	1963-83	£35-£40	$50-$60	_____	_____	☐
Small	6580	1963-83	£20-£25	$35-$45	_____	_____	☐
Miniature	6587	1963-83	£15-£20	$30-$40	_____	_____	☐

Gulliver (Designer D. Biggs)

The central character from the book, 'Gulliver's Travels', published in 1726

Large	6560	1962-67	£320-£360	$525-$575	_____	_____	☐
Small	6563	1962-67	£220-£250	$375-$400	_____	_____	☐
Miniature	6566	1962-67	£220-£260	$400-$425	_____	_____	☐

The Hampshire Cricketer (Designer H. Sales)

Limited edition of 5000

Medium	5521	To be released in 1985	_____	_____	☐

Izaac Walton (Designer H. Fenton)

The 17th Century author of 'The Compleat Angler'

Large	6404	1953-82	£35-£45	$70-$80	_____	_____	☐

Jarge (Designer H. Fenton)

Depicts a typical country bumpkin

Large	6288	1950-60	£160-£190	$200-$250	_____	_____	☐
Small	6295	1950-60	£125-£150	$200-$225	_____	_____	☐

Jester (Designer C. J. Noke)

A Royal Court comedian

Small	5556	1936-60	£45-£55	$100-$125	_____	_____	☐

Jockey (Designer D. Biggs)

A horse rider in British Horse Racing

Large	6625	1971-75	£200-£220	$180-$200	_____	_____	☐
Small	Pilot	Early 70s	Impossible to value		_____	_____	☐

John Doulton (Designer E Griffiths)

The founder of the Doulton Pottery. Issued to Collectors Club members

Version one, 8 o'clock on the clockface

Small	6656	1980	£25-£30	$35-$40	_____	_____	☐

Version two, 2 o'clock on the clockface

Small	6656	1981	£25-£30	$40-$45	_____	_____	☐

John Barleycorn (Designer C. J. Noke)

An imaginary character depicting Whiskey. Early version has the handle entering the top of the jug and is valued slightly more

Large	5327	1934-60	£65-£75	$150-$170	_____	_____	☐
Small	5735	1937-60	£45-£55	$70-$80	_____	_____	☐
Miniature	6041	1939-60	£32-£36	$65-$75	_____	_____	☐

Special Edition limited to 7500 issued in 1978

Large		1978	£65-£70	$150-$170	_____	_____	☐

John Peel (Designer H. Fenton)

A traditional English huntsman who lived for the saddle and the sound of the horn

Large	5612	1936-60	£65-£80	$140-$160	_____	_____	☐
Small	5731	1937-60	£35-£40	$70-$80	_____	_____	☐
Miniature	6130	1940-60	£30-£35	$50-$60	_____	_____	☐
Tiny	6259	1947-60	£110-£130	$240-260	_____	_____	☐

Johnny Appleseed (Designer H. Fenton)

A major American folk-lore hero

Large	6372	1953-69	£200-£225	$300-$325	_____	_____	☐

Lord Nelson (Designer M. Henk)

Depicts Admiral Lord Nelson

Large	6336	1952-69	£200-£225	$300-$325	_____	_____	☐

Lumberjack (Designer M. Henk)

Depicts a North American Lumberjack

Large	6610	1967-82	£30-£35	$70-$80	_____	_____	☐
Small	6613	1967-82	£20-£25	$40-$50	_____	_____	☐
Miniature	Pilot	Not known	£1300-£1500	$1800-$2000	_____	_____	☐
Large Canadian Centennial Backstamp							
Large	6610	1967	N.Y.D.	$180-$220	_____	_____	☐

Mad Hatter (Designer M. Henk)

A character from 'Alice's Adventures in Wonderland' by Lewis Carroll

Large	6598	1965-83	£30-£45	$50-$60	_____	_____	☐
Small	6602	1965-83	£20-£25	$40-$50	_____	_____	☐
Miniature	6606	1965-83	£15-£20	$30-$40	_____	_____	☐

Mephistopheles (Designers C. J. Noke & H. Fenton)

The devil from the medieval legend of Faust

Large	5757	1937-48	£1000-£1400	$2000-$2500	_____	_____	☐
Small	5758	1937-48	£750-£850	$900-$1000	_____	_____	☐

Mikado (Designer M. Henk)

The name is an old Japanese title for Emperor

Large	6501	1959-69	£230-£270	$375-$400	_____	_____	☐
Small	6507	1959-69	£200-£240	$300-$350	_____	_____	☐
Miniature	6522	1960-69	£220-£260	$300-$350	_____	_____	☐

Mine Host (Designer M. Henk)

A merry 'old English' Landlord

Large	6468	1958-81	£30-£45	$70-$80	_____	_____	☐
Small	6470	1958-81	£20-£25	$40-$50	_____	_____	☐
Miniature	6513	1960-81	£15-£20	$30-$40	_____	_____	☐

Monty (Early colour change version) (Designer H. Fenton)

Depicts Field Marshall Montgomery. Later versions have light yellow brown as opposed to green brown shoulders

Large	6202	1946-54	£40-£45	$70-$80	_____	_____	☐

Mr Micawber (Designers L. Harradine & H. Fenton)

A character from Charles Dickens' book, 'David Copperfield'

Intermediate	5843	1938-48	£85-£95	$160-$190	_____	_____	☐
Small	5843	1948-60	£35-£40	$95-$105	_____	_____	☐
Miniature	6138	1940-60	£30-£35	$55-$65	_____	_____	☐
Tiny	6143	1940-60	£55-£60	$130-$140	_____	_____	☐
					_____	_____	☐

Mr Pickwick (Designers L. Harradine & H. Fenton)

Another Charles Dickens character

Large	6060	1940-60	£65-£90	$140-$150	_____	_____	☐
Intermediate	5839	1938-48	£85-£95	$180-$200	_____	_____	☐
Small	5839	1948-60	£38-£43	$75-$85	_____	_____	☐
Miniature	6254	1947-60	£28-£35	$60-$70	_____	_____	☐
Tiny	6260	1947-60	£85-£95	$210-$230	_____	_____	☐

Small Pick Kwick Advertising Jug limited to 2000

Whisky bottle handle	1981	£60-£70	$100-$120	_____	_____	☐
Jim Beam handle	1983	£60-£70	$100-$120	_____	_____	☐

Night Watchman (Designer M. Henk)

A Williamsburg Series character

Large	6569	1963-83	£30-£35	$50-$60	_____	_____	☐
Small	6576	1963-83	£20-£25	$40-$50	_____	_____	☐
Miniature	6583	1963-83	£15-£20	$30-$40	_____	_____	☐

North American Indian (Canadian Centennial)

(Designer M. Henk)
Depicts the chief of the Blackfoot Tribe issued with a speical backstamp for the Canadian Centennial

Large	6611	1967	Not Known on the market	$180-$220	_____	_____	☐

Old Charley (Designer C. J. Noke)

An 18th Century nightwatchman

Large	5420	1934-83	£35-£40	$70-$80	_____	_____	☐
Small	5527	1935-83	£20-£25	$50-$60	_____	_____	☐
Miniature	6046	1939-83	£15-£20	$40-$50	_____	_____	☐
Tiny	6144	1940-60	£55-£65	$115-$125	_____	_____	☐

Old King Cole (Designer H. Fenton)

From the 'Merry Old Soul' nursery rhyme, early versions have a yellow crown and grey white hair

Large	6103	1939-60	£110-£130	$225-$250	_____	_____	☐
Small	6037	1939-60	£55-£70	$100-$120	_____	_____	☐
Lge yellow Crown		1939-40	£800-£1000	$2000-$3000	_____	_____	☐
Sml yellow Crown		1939-40	£2000-£2500	$5000-$7000	_____	_____	☐

Paddy (Designer H. Fenton)

Depicts an Irishman from old English ballads and songs

Large	5753	1937-60	£65-£75	$135-$150	_____	_____	☐
Small	5768	1937-60	£35-£40	$60-$70	_____	_____	☐
Miniature	6042	1939-60	£28-£33	$45-$55	_____	_____	☐
Tiny	6145	1940-60	£55-£65	$115-$125	_____	_____	☐

Parson Brown (Designer C. J. Noke)

An eighteenth century Anglican Parson

Large	5486	1935-60	£65-£85	$120-$140	_____	_____	☐
Small	5529	1935-60	£40-£45	$60-$70	_____	_____	☐

Pearly Boy (Designer H. Fenton)

An early version of 'Arry

Brown						
Large	1947-	£500-£800	$850-$950	_____	_____	☐
Small	1947-	£400-£500	$550-$650	_____	_____	☐
Miniature	1947-	£250-£300	$400-$500	_____	_____	☐

Blue (Tentative values only, an exceptionally rare jug)						
Large	1947-	£2500-£3000	$3500-$4500	_____	_____	☐
Small	1947-	£1400-£1600	$3000-$3500	_____	_____	☐
Miniature	1947-	£1400-£1600	$3000-$3500	_____	_____	☐

Pearly Girl (Designer H. Fenton)

An early version of 'Arriet
This piece is so rare that its value is impossible to estimate.

Pied Piper (Designer M. Henk)

A character based on medieval legend

Large	6403	1954-80	£35-£45	$70-$80	_____	_____	☐
Small	6462	1957-80	£25-£30	$50-$60	_____	_____	☐
Miniature	6514	1960-80	£20-£25	$40-$50	_____	_____	☐

Punch and Judy Man (Designer D. Biggs)

A character based on medieval legend

Large	6590	1964-69	£340-£380	$525-$550	_____	_____	☐
Small	6593	1964-69	£220-£280	$400-$450	_____	_____	☐
Miniature	6596	1964-69	£220-£280	$400-$450	_____	_____	☐

Regency Beau (Designer D. Biggs)

An Eighteenth Century 'dandy', the prince of good taste and fashion

Large	6559	1962-67	£500-£700	$1000-1500	_____	_____	☐
Small	6562	1962-67	£300-£600	$500-$550	_____	_____	☐
Miniature	6565	1962-67	£400-£600	$750-$800	_____	_____	☐

Robin Hood (First Version) (Designer M. Fenton)

The hero from the medieval legend romanticised as having robbed from the rich to give to the poor

Large	6205	1947-60	£65-£75	$140-$150	_____	_____	☐
Small	6234	1947-60	£35-£45	$70-$80	_____	_____	☐
Miniature	6252	1947-60	£35-£40	$65-$70	_____	_____	☐

Robinson Crusoe (Designer M. Henk)

Based on Daniel Defoe's character, 'Robinson Crusoe'

Large	6532	1960-82	£30-£45	$65-$75	_____	_____	☐
Small	6539	1964-82	£20-£25	$40-$50	_____	_____	☐
Miniature	6546	1964-82	£15-£20	$30-$40	_____	_____	☐

Ronald Reagan (Designer E. Griffiths)

The current President of the USA. Special limited edition of 5000 not yet sold out.

Large	6718	1984	Initial issue price $500	_____	☐

Sairey Gamp (Designers L. Harradine & H. Fenton)

A naughty nurse in Charles Dickens' Martin Chuzzlewit

Tiny	6146	1940-60	£55-£65	$100-$115	_____	☐

Samuel Johnson (Designer H. Fenton)

An eighteenth century English writer

Large	6289	1950-60	£220-£260	$275-$325	_____	☐
Small	6296	1950-60	£120-£150	$180-$200	_____	☐

Sam Weller (Designers L. Harradine & H. Fenton)
A Charles Dickens character from the 'Pickwick Papers'

Large	6064	1940-60	£70-£85	$140-$150	_____	_____	☐
Intermediate	5841	1938-48	£85-£95	$180-$200	_____	_____	☐
Small	5841	1948-60	£35-£40	$70-$80	_____	_____	☐
Miniature	6140	1940-60	£30-£35	$60-$70	_____	_____	☐
Tiny	6147	1940-60	£60-£70	$115-$125	_____	_____	☐

Sancho Panza (Designer G. Blower)
A character from the novel, 'Don Quixote'

Large	6456	1957-82	£35-£45	$75-$85	_____	_____	☐
Small	6461	1957-82	£22-£27	$40-$50	_____	_____	☐
Miniature	6518	1960-82	£17-£22	$35-$40	_____	_____	☐

Santa Claus
Good old Father Christmas

Doll Handle

Large	1981	£40-£45	$70-$80	_____	_____	☐

Reindeer Handle

Large	1982	£35-£40	$65-75	_____	_____	☐

Sack of Toys Handle

Large	1983	£30-£35	$65-75	_____	_____	☐

Scaramouche (Designer M. Henk)
A character in the novel, 'Commedia del'Arte'

Large	6558	1962-67	£400-£450	$575-$600	_____	_____	☐
Small	6561	1962-67	£260-£320	$375-$400	_____	_____	☐
Miniature	6564	1962-67	£320-£380	$400-$500	_____	_____	☐

Simple Simon (Designer M. Henk)
A character from the rhyme of the same name

Large	6374	1953-60	£300-£330	$500-$525	_____	_____	☐

Simon the Cellarer (Designers C J. Noke & H. Fenton)
A wine-cellarer from a 19th century drinking song

Large	5504	1935-60	£65-£85	$100-$125	_____	_____	☐
Small	5616	1935-60	£40-£45	$65-$75	_____	_____	☐

Smuggler (Designer D. Biggs)

Another eighteenth century British character

Large	6616	1968-80	£35-£40	$70-$80	_____	_____	☐
Small	6619	1968-80	£25-£30	$45-$55	_____	_____	☐
Miniature	Pilot	1968	£1400-£1600	$2000-$2500	_____	_____	☐

Smuts (Designer H. Fenton)

Jan Christian Smuts (1870-1950), a South African Statesman

Large	6198	1946-48	£950-£1200	$1800-$2200	_____	_____	☐

St. George (Designer M. Henk)

The patron saint of England

Large	6618	1968-75	£75-£95	$170-$190	_____	_____	☐
Small	6621	1968-75	£65-£75	$90-$110	_____	_____	☐

Tam O'Shanter (Designer M. Henk)

A central character in the Robert Burns poem of the same name

Large	6632	1973-79	£35-£45	$70-$80	_____	_____	☐
Small	6636	1973-79	£20-£25	$50-$60	_____	_____	☐
Miniature	6640	1973-79	£18-£23	$40-$50	_____	_____	☐

Toby Philpots (Designer C. J. Noke)

Based on Toby Fillpot, a jovial eighteenth century drinker

Large	5736	1937-69	£60-£75	$140-$160	_____	_____	☐
Small	5737	1937-69	£33-£38	$70-$80	_____	_____	☐
Miniature	6043	1937-69	£26-£32	$45-$55	_____	_____	☐

Tony Weller (Designers L. Harradine & H. Fenton)

The father of Sam Weller in Dickens' Pickwick Papers

Extra Large		1936-	£120-£150	$225-$250	_____	_____	☐
Large	5531	1936-60	£65-£70	$140-$150	_____	_____	☐
Small	5530	1936-60	£35-£40	$70-$80	_____	_____	☐
Miniature	6044	1939-60	£30-£35	$60-$70	_____	_____	☐

Touchstone (Designer C. J. Noke)

A clown in Shakespeare's 'As You Like It'

Large	5613	1936-60	£100-£140	$200-$275	_____	_____	☐

Town Crier (Designer D. Biggs)

A medieval news announcer

Large	6530	1960-73	£110-£130	$180-$225	_____	_____	☐
Small	6537	1960-73	£65-£75	$100-$120	_____	_____	☐
Miniature	6544	1960-73	£80-£90	$110-$130	_____	_____	☐

Trapper (Designers M. Henk & D. Biggs)

An early North American fur hunter

Large	6609	1967-82	£35-£45	$70-$80	_____	_____	☐
Small	6612	1967-82	£20-£25	$45-$55	_____	_____	☐
Miniature	Pilot	1967-68	£1400-£1600	$2000-$2500	_____	_____	☐
Large Centennial Backstamp							
Large	6609	1967	Not known on the market	$180-$220	_____	_____	☐

Ugly Duchess (Designer M. Henk)

Another character from 'Alice in Wonderland'

Large	6659	1965-73	£260-£300	$400-$425	_____	_____	☐
Small	6603	1965-73	£220-£240	$250-$300	_____	_____	☐
Miniature	6607	1965-73	£220-£240	$250-$300	_____	_____	☐

Uncle Tom Cobbleigh (Designer M. Henk)

A character from a song in 1800 about Widdecombe Fair

Large	6337	1952-60	£200-£225	$400-$425	_____	_____	☐

Vicar of Bray (Designers C. J. Noke & H. Fenton)

A character from a song sung during the reign of George I

Large	5615	1936-60	£120-£140	$190-$210	_____	_____	☐

Viking (Designer M. Henk)

A Scandinavian explorer/warrior

Large	6496	1959-75	£85-£100	$120-$140	_____	_____	☐
Small	6502	1959-75	£65-£75	$100-120	_____	_____	☐
Miniature	6525	1960-75	£60-£75	$120-$140	_____	_____	☐

Veteran Motorist (Designer D. Biggs)

A character representing one of the first motorists

Large	6633	1973-83	£35-£40	$50-$60	_____	_____	☐
Small	6637	1973-83	£25-£30	$40-$50	_____	_____	☐
Miniature	6641	1973-83	£20-£25	$35-$40	_____	_____	☐

Walrus and Carpenter (Designer M. Henk)

Based on Lewis Carroll's 'Through the Looking-Glass' published 1872

Large	6600	1965-79	£35-£45	$80-$90	_____	_____	⊏
Small	6604	1965-79	£20-£25	$55-$65	_____	_____	⊏
Miniature	6608	1965-79	£15-£20	$40-$50	_____	_____	⊏

Yachtsman (Designer D. Biggs)

Inspired by Sir Francis Chichester's circumnavigation

Large	6622	1971-79	£35-£45	$90-$100	_____	_____	⊏
Small	Pilot	1971	£1200-£1500	$2000-$2500	_____	_____	⊏
Miniature	Pilot	1971	£1200-£1500	$2000-$2500	_____	_____	⊏

Collectors Top Ten

The first edition of this book carried a reply card which invited collectors to list their favourite ten character jugs. All the reply cards received have been used to determine a collectors top ten by adding up all the 'votes' cast for each character. A few characters received equal number of votes and therefore share an equal chart position.

1. Mephistopheles
2. Ugly Duchess
3. Regency Beau
4. Gardener
5. Mr. Pickwick
   Gulliver
   John Peel

6. Captain Hook
7. Gladiator
   Dick Whittington
8. Walrus & Carpenter
9. Smuts
10. Old Charley

The front and back view of the collectors favourite, The Mephistopheles. Numbers two and three in our collectors survey, The Ugly Duchess and Regency Beau.

The Old Tinies

Auld Mac	£110-£130	$225-$250	☐
John Peel	£110-£130	$240-$260	☐
Cardinal	£110-£120	$225-$250	☐
Mr Pickwick	£85-£95	$210-$230	☐
'Arry	£80-£90	$200-$225	☐
'Arriet	£80-£90	$200-$225	☐
Mr Micawber	£55-£60	$130-$140	☐
Sam Weller	£60-£70	$115-$125	☐
Fat Boy	£55-£65	$130-$140	☐
Old Charley	£55-£65	$115-$125	☐
Paddy	£55-£65	$115-$125	☐
Sairey Gamp	£55-£65	$100-$115	☐
Full Tinies Set	£1000-£1200	$1800-$2000	

The original 12 tinies.

The Modern Tinies

These jugs are the same size as the "Old Tinies" (1½ inches tall) and only twelve characters have been produced. They were sold by subscription only at a rate of one a month ending in December 1982. Originally sold at £12.50 sterling they are valued now on the British market at £25-£30 each and $30-$40 on the American market. The reason for such an increase is their relative scarcity on the market as few collectors are willing to part with their own collection.

The following characters were made.

Character	Designer
Mr Bumble	Robert Tabbenor
Fagin	Robert Tabbenor
Uriah Heep	Robert Tabbenor
Mrs Bardell	Robert Tabbenor
Oliver Twist	Robert Tabbenor
Betsy Trotwood	Michael Abberley
Bill Sykes	Michael Abberley
Scrooge	Michael Abberley
David Copperfield	Michael Abberley
Little Nell	Michael Abberley
Artful Dodger	Peter Gee
Dickens	Eric J Griffiths

Full Modern Tinies Set   £300-£360 $360-$480

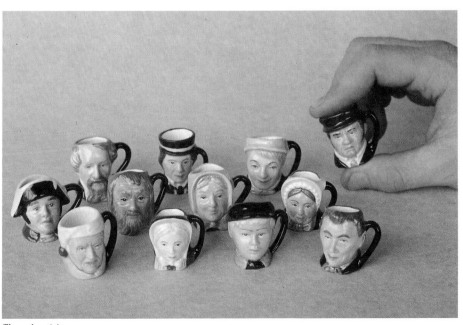

The modern tinies.

Doulton Toby Jugs

Doulton Toby Jugs, which in recent years have been overshadowed by the interest in character jugs, are likewise collected by enthusiasts worldwide. As is the rule in character jugs, discontinued Tobys are worth considerably more than their current counterparts.

Many Doulton character jugs are represented in Doulton Toby form as well. One character jug which causes disappointment to those who don't realise that it comes in two forms is the Winston Churchill. Only a few white Churchill character jugs exist compared with the thousands of Toby Churchills produced and sold worldwide. My dealer contacts regularly have people telephoning them to ask, "Which Churchill is the rare one?" Hopefully one day someone will not be disappointed with the answer they get.

Discontinued Toby Jugs

Character	Production Dates	Size		
Best is not too good	1939-60	4½"	£120-£140	$250-$275
Capt Cuttle	1948-60	4½"	£90-£110	$180-$200
Double XX	1939-69	6½"	£150-£175	$330-$350
Fat Boy	1948-60	4½"	£90-£110	$180-$200
Mr Micawber	1948-60	4½"	£90-£110	$180-$200
Mr Pickwick	1948-60	4½"	£90-£110	$180-$200
Old Charley	1939-60	5½"	£90-£110	$180-$200
Old Charley	1939-60	8¾"	£110-£130	$225-$250
Sairey Gamp	1948-60	4½"	£90-£110	$180-$200
Sam Weller	1948-60	4½"	£90-£110	$180-$200
The Squire	1950-69	6"	£100-£120	$250-$275

The six Doulton Dickens' Tobies worth £90-£110 or $180-$200 each.

Current Toby Jugs

Large	*Small*	*Medium*
Falstaff	Happy John	Jolly Toby
Happy John	Honest Measure	Winston Churchill
Huntsman	Falstaff	
Sherlock Holmes	Winston Churchill	
Sir Francis Drake		
Winston Churchill		

The three large Cliff Cornell Toby jugs.

Cliff Cornell Toby Jug

These jugs were produced in 1956 for an American industrialist called Cliff Cornell. They were used as gifts to his friends and customers. In all versions of the jug the base carries the following inscription

> *Greetings*
> *Cliff Cornell*
> *Famous Cornell Fluxes*
> *Cleveland Flux Company*

The jugs were produced in three colours brown, blue and tan and in two sizes, 9 inches and 5½ inches. The tan version is considerably rarer than the brown and blue versions. The production run for the brown and blue jugs has been reported as being 500 jugs for each large version and 375 for each of the smaller versions. Production figures for the tan variations are unknown but are certainly far lower. Market Value:

	Brown		Blue		Tan	
Large	£300-£325	$325-$350	£300-£325	$325-$350	£450-£500	$500-$525
Small	£325-£350	$350-$375	£275-£300	$300-$325	Unknown	

Charrington

This 9¼ inch Toby was made in the 1950's to advertise Charrington Ale. It was previously thought that only two versions existed; however, the Collectors' Club have, in the last year, identified a third version. The three versions are identifiable by differences in the wording on the front and side of the jug. The newly discovered version says 'Toby' on the front and just 'Charrrington' on the side, Whilst the other two common versions say 'Toby Ale' in block letters on one and 'One Toby leads to Another' in script on the other.

Market Value:
Common versions: £80-£90/$300-$350
Rare versions: not known/not known

George Robey

An extremely rare early Doulton Toby made during the 1920s. It has a cover in the form of a hat, the absence of which would reduce its market value.

Market Value:
£4000-£5000/$8000-$8500

Early Huntsman

In 1963 an early Huntsman with a silver rein and different colours on the body was found. It was dated for 1919 nearly twenty years prior to the current Huntsman introductions. This jug was sold in auction for £300 in 1983. Its value on todays market would be considerably more.

Charlie Chaplin

Another extremely rare early Doulton Toby made during the 1920s. It also has a cover in the form of a hat.

Market Value:
£4000-£5000/$8000-$8500

The Charlie Chaplin Toby jug.

Miscellaneous Wares

Royal Doulton has also produced a range of other wares based on certain character jugs:

Extra Large Size

The only reported jug of this size is Tony Weller. It is approximately one inch higher than the large size Tony Weller and noticeably wider at the top.
Market Value: £120-£150 $225-$250

Mini-Busts

These are a series of busts manufactured between 1939 and 1960. Only six characters were manufactured, all of whom where Dickens' characters. They were made with both square and oval bases.

Character	Market Value	
Buz Fuz	£35-£45	$90-$100
Mr Micawber	£35-£45	$90-$100
Mr Pickwick	£35-£45	$90-$100
Sairey Gamp	£35-£45	$90-$100
Sam Weller	£35-£45	$90-$100
Tony Weller	£35-£45	$90-$100

Liqueur Containers

These are small size jugs, whose tops have a small round opening for cork stoppers. The presence of their original contents will increase the price of this jug.

Falstaff	£40-£50	$100-$120
Poacher	£40-£50	$100-$120
Rip Van Winkle	£40-£50	$100-$120

Cigarette Lighters

These were first produced by Royal Doulton in 1958 and only 14 characters in a small size were used. Prior to this a company in America, who had a Doulton dealership converted some small character jugs into lighters. This was done by filling them with plaster of paris, painting it black and inserting a lighter mechanism in the top. These converted jugs are not listed in this booklet and the following list only lists those made by Royal Doulton.

Bacchus	1964-74	£65-£75	$140-$160
Beefeater	1967-74	£60-£70	$110-$120
Buz Fuz	1958-59	£80-£100	$200-$225
Captain Ahab	1964-74	£65-£75	$140-$150
Captain Cuttle	1958-59	£90-£110	$200-$225
Falstaff	1958-74	£65-£75	$110-$120
Lawyer	1962-74	£65-£75	$120-$140
Long John Silver	1958-73	£65-£75	$110-$120
Mr Micawber	1958-59	£80-£100	$200-$225
Mr Pickwick	1958-62	£75-£95	$190-$210
Musketeer (Porthos)	1958-59	£170-£200	$425-$475
Old Charley	1958-74	£65-£75	$110-$120
Poacher	1958-74	£65-£75	$110-$120
Rip Van Winkle	1958	£170-£200	$425-$475

Ashtrays

These are miniature jugs whose bases are attached to a black bowl. There were only four characters used and they have no difference in market value between them. All were made between 1936 and 1960.

Dick Turpin	£55-£75	$100-$125
John Barleycorn	£55-£75	$100-$125
Old Charley	£55-£75	$100-$125
Parson Brown	£55-£75	$100-$125

Ash Pots/Ash Bowls

These are small character jugs with an internally overhanging top lid. This top lid may have one or two grooves in it to rest cigarettes. They were all made between 1939 and 1960.

Auld Mac	£55-£75	$100-$125
Farmer John	£55-£75	$100-$125
Old Charley	£55-£75	$100-$125
Paddy	£55-£75	$100-$125
Parson Brown	£55-£75	$100-$125
Sairey Gamp	£55-£75	$100-$125

The four Ash trays.

The six Ash pots/bowls.

Napkin Rings

These were made between 1939 and 1960 mainly for the USA market. They rarely appear on the UK market and only seldom on the USA market. Looking like mini busts set on porcelain napkin rings they were only made in six Dickens' characters and occasionally turn up in a gift pack.

Fat Boy	£170-£200	$350-$375
Mr Micawber	£170-£200	$350-$375
Mr Pickwick	£170-£200	$350-$375
Sairey Gamp	£170-£200	$350-$375
Sam Weller	£170-£200	$350-$375
Tony Weller	£170-£200	$350-$375

Tobacco Jars

These are large jugs manufactured with a metal insert in the top to house the cover mechanism. There were only made in two characters between 1938 and 1960.

Old Charley	£200-£250	$550-$600
Paddy	£180-£220	$500-$600

The front and base view of the Auld Mac musical jug.

Musical Character Jugs

These are large character jugs with a musical box and key built into their base. When wound and lifted off the surface they will play a tune. They are believed to have been made between 1938 and 1945.

Character	Tune Played	Market Value	
Auld Mac	The Campbells are Coming	£400-£500	$700-$800
Old Charlie	Have a Health to His Majesty	£450-£550	$700-$800
Old King Cole	Old King Cole Was A Merry Old Soul	£500-£600	$1700-$2100
Paddy	An Irish Jig	£400-£500	$700-$800
Tony Weller	Come Landlord Fill the Flowing Bowl	£400-£500	$700-$800

Dickens Jugs and Tankards

These six jugs and one tankard, while not strictly speaking character jugs, are derivatives and are collected by jug enthusiasts. They all have a raised relief which depicts various Dickens' characters and scenes.

Old London	1949-60	£90-£110	$270-$300
Peggatty	1944-60	£90-£110	$270-$300
Old Curiosity Shop	1935-60	£60-£80	$130-$150
Pickwick Papers	1937-60	£60-£80	$130-$150
Oliver Twist	1936-60	£60-£80	$130-$150
Oliver Asks for More	1949-60	£70-£90	$250-$270
Oliver Twist Tankard	1949-60	£70-£90	$250-$270

Future Editions

It is the intention of the publishers to produce a third edition of this book in 1986. In this forthcoming edition all prices will be revised and updated. In addition to this it is hoped to include photographs and information submitted by collectors. Collectors who would like to contribute photographs or articles about character jugs should contact the author via the publisher's address. Any collector who wishes to buy, sell or swop particular jugs can also advertise in next years edition. Simply tick the indicated box on the reply card and details on advertising will be sent prior to publication.

Recommended Reading

Character Jugs
Royal Doulton Character and Toby Jugs by Desmond Eyles
Character Jug Collecting by Syd Gardner
A Revised Price Guide to the Royal Doulton Discontinued Character Jugs (USA version) By Princess & Barry Weiss
Collecting Royal Doulton Character & Toby Jugs by Jocelyn Lukins

Other Doulton Works
Royal Doulton Series Ware by Louise Irvine
Limited Edition Loving Cups and Jugs by Richard Dennis
Royal Doulton Figures by Desmond Eyles and Richard Dennis
The Doulton Story by Paul Attersbury and Louise Irvine
Doulton Flambe Animals by Jocelyn Lukins
Royal Doulton Figures by Chilton Press
The Doulton Lambeth Ware by Desmond Eyles
The Price Guide to the Complete Royal Doulton Figurine Collection by Mary Lou Yeager

To be published soon
The Doulton Figures Collectors Handbook by Kevin Pearson